AF243813

Cast Your Eyes Like Riverstones Into The Exquisite Dark

by Danny Sherrard

Write Bloody Publishing

writebloody.com

Copyright © Danny Sherrard, 2025.

All rights reserved. No part of this book may be used, performed, or reproduced in any manner whatsoever without written permission from the publisher except in the case of brief quotations embodied in critical articles or reviews.

First edition.
ISBN: 978-0982148846

Cover Design by Derrick C. Brown
Interior Layout by Nikki Steele
Edited by Derrick C. Brown
Proofread by Haley Hutchinson
Author Photo by Madelyn Hollister

Type set in Bergamo.

Printed in the USA

Write Bloody Publishing
Los Angeles, CA

Support Independent Presses
writebloody.com

This book is for B. Wakefield

Who never gave up on me,

Who beat the path so I could run it

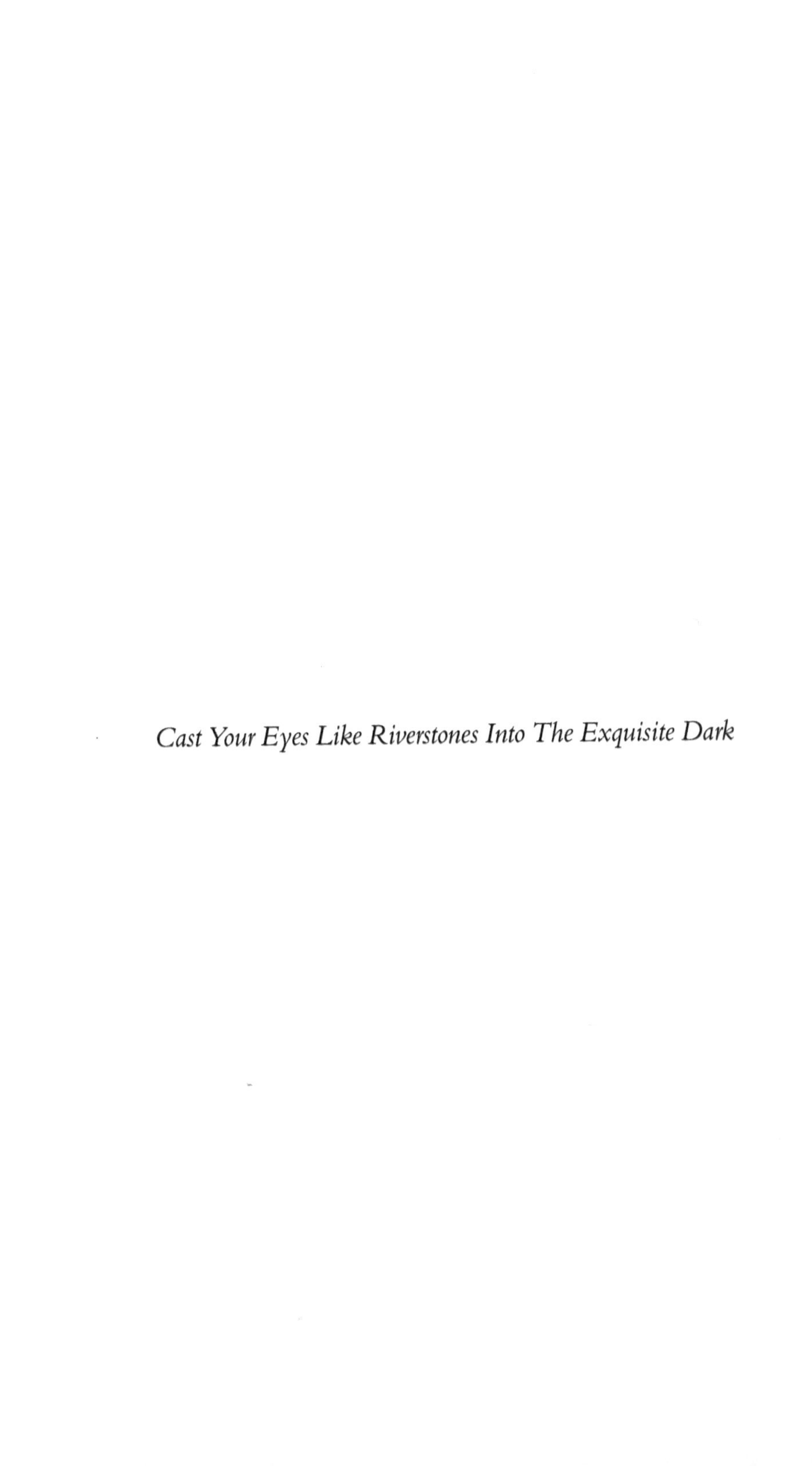

Cast Your Eyes Like Riverstones Into The Exquisite Dark

CAST YOUR EYES LIKE RIVERSTONES INTO THE EXQUISITE DARK

I.
Momenta

II.
Wolf Whelp

III.
Mythos

IV.
Love As Lightning

V.

Nostos

"One's life, from being an exterior thing, grows inwards. Its intensity stays the same; and, d'you know, it's most mysterious, the corners in which the joy of living can sometimes hide away."

—Blaise Cendrars

Author's Note

In the fall of 2003, my dear friend Chris Carroll painted a giant eye on my bedroom wall. He then depicted a waterfall surging from the eye's amethyst iris. Adrift within the blue waterfall, he rendered three pyramids and wrote the words,

The Places I Have Been Will Visit Me Once Again

Then we met once or twice a week upstairs at Seattle's Cafe Allegro to write together. Hungrily passing an exquisite corpse or a new book between our hands, I failed to realize how the words in Chris's painting would impact me years later. I see them now as divinatory, just as I imagine Chris knew they were when he composed them.

I once wanted to be an astronaut and a witch doctor. I wanted to join a traveling carnival. I never dared hope that poetry would become the catalyst spiriting me away across the world and, in some sense, beyond the world since poetry will teach you to regard most things in an altogether different light.

I am honored to be a part of a generation unafraid to stare into the void, into the abyss, and pull from it the secrets and the answers that make us live. My eternal gratitude goes to those who have pulled me out of that self-same abyss when I needed it most.

To the Hero of My Tomorrow,
to the Little Bird,
and to the Wish Detectives,

May The Places I Have Been Visit Me Once Again.

–Danny Sherrard
February 26th, 2009
Silver City, New Mexico

NOTE TO THE SECOND EDITION

Metamorphosis embodied the theme of the past year, so when Write Bloody asked if I'd be interested in "resurrecting" this collection of poems, it made a kind of cosmic sense. Transforming the structure of this collection developed into a process as curative as it was serendipitous. We discovered the occurrence of a fluke: in translation from one printer to another, the original file containing the old edition had vanished. Thus, the opportunity to shed some weary texts, transmute others, and, via newer writing, amplify the content of this book unveiled itself. Metamorphosis activated, I set to work, holding deep gratitude to the good folks at Write Bloody for this gift.

The texts we cut flowered their last blossoms long ago, and their removal augments the vitality of this book.

Many of the pieces remaining from the first edition were composed during a time of upheaval, chaos, and suffering. Someone told me that an object in motion possesses no location, so I resolved to stay in motion for as long as possible. I felt that by running, I could shed my suffering like a husk whose strands were attached to my being, and if I stayed in motion long enough, I'd eventually unshackle myself from it. The notion proved infeasible (the road wrapped its cocoon around me until stillness settled in), but the poems that emerged from testing the hypothesis are fragments of a mirror that reflect the moon or youthful audacity or a fleeting prayer. In going back through these pieces, I learned what I ran from was, in fact, the most profound teacher for whom one could hope. In reworking these old poems, it is heartening to realize, without a shadow of a doubt, that I've stopped running from that teacher. And, in drawing closer to various *lessons*, perhaps I've managed to aim these pieces of shattered mirror ever more skyward.

The new poems that found their way into this edition seemed to me ones whose tonal, thematic, or synesthetic qualities melded seamlessly with the collection's previous dreamscape: one of these, *Riverstone*, emphasizes surrender; another, a single tablet from my rendering of the *Gilgamesh Epic*, is about a journey. If given the task of summing up what this collection of poems expounds on, I might say, "It is about surrendering to the journey."

And, it occurs to me that this is what metamorphosis is likewise about,
for you must surrender your being–the places you have been, the stories
that compose you, and the memory that ripples through it all–to the
process of transformation and then you must emerge from the chrysalis
anew, so the world may witness how the magic from before has rewoven
itself to dance through your wingspan now.

–Danny Sherrard
October 15th, 2024
Florence, Italy

CHAPTER I
MOMENTA

RIVERSTONE

Weather-etched echo sculptor,
as star stuff gathered into the semblance of your stillness,
and later, torchlight shimmered across ochre-painted
megafauna galloping upon your cave walls,
you, offshoot hewn from the herd of eternal shapes,
continued your migration through cosmos and continental drift.

As mist and moth wing began to bear your hue,
you, nautilus of time, fossilized apocalypses
and drowned death in the depths of your memory,
that fog-carved chrysalis
in which chrysanthemum-colored rocks blossom.

In you dwells the spirit of a great mountain,
a nimble spirit greeting those who sojourn
in your wayfarer's fane. Dreaming
of adz and wall, ripple, of caryatid,
meteorite, anchor, and of crumbling wall.

Surrendering to the living hand
you cleave the colossus.
Yielding to the river pulverizes you
into a pantheon of prayer.

SIRIUS

I don't know when the dog started barking at me.
The possibility the dog has barked at me the entire time
I've lived in this rough apartment exists.

A chain link fence contains the sunken
house across the street from where I catch the bus.
The skeleton of a trampoline dissolves each day
behind that fence. Somewhere from that abyss
bellows the barking of a dog who only barks at me
while I wait for my bus, or walk to the grocery store.

More often than not, I hear someone yelling at the dog
when it barks. I don't know what they're saying
but the voice is cruel. The cruel voice fails
to extinguish the broken bark.

Why do I know the dog barks only at me?
Because the behavior of the other people at the bus stop
becomes tense when I arrive. I watch their gait change.
An old, forgotten part of them stirs, and I see
their posture shift. All this makes me self-conscious
since the dog only barks at me.

I wonder if they think to themselves,
What on Earth did that person do to that dog?
Although, most likely, they're just hoping
for the dog to shut up.

The bark's frequency is not drowned out by traffic.
The bark's intensity waxes while the cruel voice wanes.
The bark is not tough, nor is it weak.
I might call it virile, I might call it brave.
I think the dog is in trouble and has chosen me
to help it escape. I think the dog, if I did try
and rescue it, might try to rip me to shreds.

I cannot place its breed by the timbre of the bark
despite how many images I conjure, though I know it
is not a pug. The dog is not a pug or a Pomeranian

or anything you might call cute. The dog is lean,
underfed, and ruthless. The dog is not a purebred,
but it desires the wild, to possess the pure while
possessed by the wild.

Desperately, this dog runs in his sleep.
In his sleep, he dreams of a pack of wild
dogs he's never seen before.
He dreams he is one of them.
In the dreams of this dog, he speaks
not a language of barks,
but of howls, of wind
direction of hunt. This dog howls
in his dreams with his pack.
Their sinews blaze,
their fur thick as night rain
moonlit, soaked
and snow-swept, cascading
Promethean through the mist,
loyal and alert. Dozing,
they sleep in circles
that look like one rippling paw,
a breathing ancestral glacier,
primordial and star-strewn. Dark,
alive. When this dog awakens, he paces.
And when I approach, he barks at me.

TORMENTA

The pregnant sky darkened
as if the Earth's journey skipped a beat
toward night or an eclipse
behind the clouds
the clouds gathered
in sudden electric telepathy
daylight shatters
and a handful of blue
droplets flow a rosary
wound around your wrist
while windows latch
inside the Bougainvillea
inside the clandestine courtyards
the gentle tantrum of a theater
after the lights dim
before the curtains open
the moment that births the storm

INCANDESCENCE

When the lightning struck,
my eyes saw my veins radiate
like the white coils of neon signs.
The signs were in gibberish.
Otherwise, I'd tell you what they said.

When I woke up,
I smelled rain and fire and water-soaked earth.
I smelled cement. A hand
pressed like a river
into the bed of my back.
I heard a woman asking
if I was there. The woman told me
she could see my bones.
She told me she'd called an ambulance.

When I got home from the hospital
the next morning, my roommate,
Leopold, noticed my limp
and, after hearing what transpired, suggested
that I rest. He also handed me some Aloe Vera
for my burnt leg.

I remember not being afraid yet.
I remember feeling a sense of levity
because I knew surviving
a lightning bolt was no small feat.
Looking back, I see I was placed
inside a blur or daze.
Thoughts and emotions seemed far away
like a mirror that gives no reflection,
only *mirrorness*.

I slept for a day and the next morning
I noticed no change
until I found my hair falling out in clumps.
The doctor hadn't warned me about this,
but the thought of returning
to the hospital didn't cross my mind.

Given what followed
I probably should've looked
for outside assistance, a support group.

It has been more than a decade now
and I can finally write about it
with more solace and thoughtfulness.

In the immediate wake of being struck
I noticed a number of aftereffects:

    1.   My dreams began to seem slower.
    2.   I attained night tremors.
    3.   My vision became strange, blurry.
    4.   Dislocation from time and space, like a species of vertigo.
    5.   Short-term memory loss.
    6.   Sudden jolts of fear or anguish.
    7.   On occasion, I would see people who do not exist.

After researching these phenomena, I've found
they parallel the experience of other survivors
of lightning strikes. I also believe that I discovered
why lightning struck me and, perhaps, how I survived.

I was wearing big headphones and walking
through a thunderstorm, listening to music.
I'm from a city of rain, not lightning—
the notion of getting struck never crossed
my mind. The headphones' metallic bridge
functioned as a weathervane, making
my body a conductor for the lightning to
travel through. Both of my feet must have
been on the ground, post-mid-step, and I
was wearing Chuck Taylors which have
rubber soles.

I don't remember falling.

PAUPER

Give me the word for staring down
your reflection until it backs up & walks away.
Give me the word for squeezing your shadow
into a mop bucket.

Make the word *chaos* a palindrome
or always spell it incorrectly?

Give me the word for how your calves feel
after running through a dream.

What is the word again?

The word for the boxes in which you move yourself?

Raindrunk is a word.

What *is* the word?

Something like the word
for how space always ends
with the forging of a fist
just as it begins
with a single hand
unraveling
toward you.

DELPHINUS

After the whale vomited me up onto shore I changed outfits. No place
for a waiter where I wandered. I found a low branch by the forest for my
apron, that white flag. There, I deserted my center of gravity to wave
in the wind. I loosened my tie (*shoulda thoughta that in the whale*). I let it
rest like a boa around my crooked collar. I smelled like death, which is
to say, history. Arid air turning turquoise collaged my trousers to my
legs. I stripped them off like tree bark. *Coulda fashioned me a canoe out of it
and dipped. Coulda Houdinied again:* it's only ever a scotch, gin, and a rum
away. (The whale swallows mouthfuls of you.) To hell with the collar and
tie. I left them on the ground like broken cocoons. Terrestrial creatures
approached and sniffed my shed skin. Then they backed away with their
paws up. I began to hear the murmuring of pitter-patter. I imagined a
colossal mantis or troglodyte, transparent, made of the shape of rain,
drumming the raindrops ever closer to me from the distance. Then
the rain rolled in and consumed me, its sudden rivers swept away the
leviathan-viscera. My whole being danced in the forest, ecstatic and free,
leaping tree branch-high.

CHAPTER II
WOLF WHELP

AFTERSPEAK

Before talk,
I memorized the way
home, through the car window.
October leaves, world scent.
Whirled rain shadow. Gray green.
Setting to memory
direction & location
kept inside the silence
of knowing that one turn
at the bottom of the hill
meant *grocery store*
and two meant *meadow, stadium.*
I remember also the odd route
occurring, the unfamiliar
road to the doctor's office
where they tried to determine
what was wrong with me,
why a child of almost four years
seemed unable to speak.
And I remember one
of my first words:
Mufferdoo.

I was trying to say the word *comfortable.*

I was trying to say, *I'm comfortable*
here. Right here. Inside this silence
before the world leaves.

KINDERGARTEN

I have pinpointed the precise moment I stopped wanting to learn in a classroom atmosphere: it was in kindergarten when they tried to make me think like everyone else. You see, I'd been drawing God with crayons. I gave him fountain fingers, mountains, and rainbow tears. Strictly mystical, he was in a childlike daze.

God doesn't cry, my teacher told me. *He's invisible.* And she crumpled up my page.

Contemplating my new sheet of construction paper and remembering God crumpled up in the garbage can, I left this tantalizing page blank. You see, it was an exquisite sky-blue and resembled the warm September morning.

Why change that? I asked myself. It already reflected my lack of grounding.

My thoughts stormed back to God in the garbage can, and with that, I drew some dark clouds and in their middle, my name. I saw my teacher's angry glance and began to draw some rain.

My teacher sat me next to another student finishing her self-portrait. It dawned on me that the teacher meant for us to draw our faces, not what lives behind them. At that moment, it struck me how unattractive vanity is.

Next week at Sunday school, we were asked to draw God, and I thought twice before I began to draw a beautiful woman. I cried when the teacher took me outside and scolded me for sinning. It had been a heavy week.

But I kept my paintbrush feet, and on walks home from school, I would draw the seasons through themselves and imagine growing wings to escape a concrete reality. To this day, I have more to explore through the worlds I created than in this synthetic paradise that never branches trees of good and evil into my memory but only unfolds walls of chaos. Spraycan in my hand, I graffitied those walls with Nefertiti twirls, Nabatean swirls, and windowsills into the divine. All I know about these worlds of mine is that they know good and don't understand evil. They can give you more life than death, more dreams than breath. On this earthless bed of immortality, reality is the spirit in your lungs where you can lie beneath yourself to count stars and only get to one. You should find me there, and we could watch as the galaxies begin to gallop, turning into words inside ourselves to sing of freedom before nihilism eases into everything else.

Though they've wreathed our heads to mark our light when stars are dead, we contain the paint to turn the skies blue again from lack of bloodshed. And I'll resurrect these dreams to soar from the words and worlds I have read.

TORNADO MEN

So, my dad drove me to Burger Master—
this sort of greasy old restaurant with long
angular bull horns for a sign that point all
the way back to the 50's.

Older folks tend to favor it because they can find it
and it has decaf and a salad bar and everything.
I've never had the daring to try their fish filet
so I got the Burger Master with onion rings
and my dad got the same, and I paid to cushion
the foreboding topic of the day, which was
my future.

We took our plastic number and found a booth
that seemed messy, the way a change return
in a rest stop soda machine seems messy.

Time for me is more of a three-dimensional map
with topographical texture than it is a tightrope
I am walking.

Time for my dad is more like the tightrope
so it didn't surprise me when his forehead
wrinkles performed their balancing act,
or when his forehead wrinkles said to me,
Son, we are very disappointed in you.

Now by *we* his forehead wrinkles probably meant
my mom and him, and quite possibly ancestors
I've never met before. He'd picked, impeccably,
the day of my high school's graduation and at least
four months after I'd dropped out and moved
into my girlfriend's house to inform me of this,
and I, well, I had to agree with him.

My father has seen more of the world than most
people I know. He joined the Air Force, put himself
through college, and had a mental breakdown
when he found out my mom was pregnant with me.

I think I was an accident
and can appreciate that,
the way some people
can appreciate an extra limb
that isn't fully functional
or a wigged-out birthmark.

My expression told him this,
that I agreed with him,
and his head shook in bewilderment
at the fact that I was smiling and his
shaking head said to me, *Son, you look
like an extraterrestrial.* And he wasn't joking.

No, I was not stoned. But he must've thought
that I was, staring at this sideways beam of light
that is his son. His extraterrestrial son perched
like Basquiat's crown hovered over his head.

Our food descended like the parachutes of peace
and my thoughts became weathervanes calling
for the lightning of silence to strike me so I could
kindle a little clarity.

        (Yes, I was the poet laureate of my high school.
        Yes, I was probably the first poet laureate
        in the history of high schools to drop out.
        First semester of senior year, I only attended
        one class, this creative writing course taught
        by a wizened hippie with a wonder for words.
        This class wasn't even on my ordained schedule,
        I just started showing up, and I think he let me attend
        because he was on the committee that made
        me poet laureate, and I think he felt responsible for me.
        I also went to school to buy and sell marijuana.
        Neither the teacher nor my dad knew that,
        but it's how I paid for our food at Burger Master.)

Dad, I once dreamt
that two tornados chased us
after they destroyed our home.
We ran from them across the night

across the prairie
until our legs gave out.
We watched the tornados approach
but as they drew closer
they diminished
until they became slow swirling dust
devils a few feet high.
No longer tornados.
Now, two children with glowing eyes
stood still before us.
You asked in the dream
who taught them
to turn into tornados. They told us
an answer we already knew. They said
their grandfathers had taught them how.

That day, I wanted to say, *Dad, I know*
how bad it hurts to become a tornado
and the dislocation you experience
upon finding the aftermath of the world
of the home you laid to waste.

I wanted to say,
Dad, someone that powerful
is who should put the world back together,
it just requires a different sort of strength.

(But those words conjured themselves too late.)

I think my dad was expecting an all-out war
at the lunch table that day. He had the grenades
in his eyes. I don't know much about debate,
but I think it is difficult to argue with someone who
agrees with you. So, when he found me there
like Gravity's white flag stuck into the cloud I lived in,
our mannerisms reverted back to what they usually
were, like when the game's on, and it's not the playoffs yet.

Outside, I lit a cigarette.
My father told me I shouldn't smoke.
I nodded my head.
He asked if he could give me a ride

to my girlfriend's house.
I said I'd walk.
We shook hands.
I smiled.
And then we went in different directions.

THE CLAIRVOYANT GOES TO WORK

This just one of those days that he already
ate all the grapes off the grapevine,
perhaps even before rising from bed.
They turned into an acidic wine in his womb
where his inner child began wandering wine-drunk
and stumbled out into his bowl of cereal, then
out into the neighborhood painted milk.

When the clairvoyant left his house for work,
unaware of the absence of his inner child,
he heard voices in his stomach from all over
the city melding together. It sounded like Bhangra.
If this is a scene in a movie, he thought,
the soundtrack would be Bhangra. Slow
motion observations of the speed of sound.

That didn't matter.
To the clairvoyant, as he passed the banana stand,
the public multi-sex restroom, and then crossed
the avenue diagonally, what mattered was possession.
What mattered was possession. Whose *is* was whose?
For instance, he asked himself, *is that my hair
on your head, Tiny Cyclone of Leaves?
Glofish, are those* my *words you're scribbling?
And that pick-up line you're saying Rosebud,
those smoke and mirrors are most certainly* mine!

Yes, paranoia possessed our clairvoyant in the best of ways
by the time he arrived at the aquarium store.

*I haven't felt this good since
I kicked the ghost out,* he thought.

But he thought too soon,
because someone heard him
and, after an audible giggle
from the inside of one
of the empty aquariums,
that someone began to speak:
I reached down your throat

to get my heart back.
I only caught your breath.
What of bodies?
Ours now lie in ruins
amidst mountain tops.
People climb up there
looking for themselves.
Maybe all they'll see
are the apparitions of two
drunken children
dancing mist over
the edge of the world.

BUSBOY

When I worked as a busboy
I wanted to tell all the customers
something I don't believe–
I wanted to say,
Listen, there's never
gonna be enough water
to quench the world.

All the while memorizing,
Plate, small fork, big fork, napkin, knife, spoon, glass
Plate, smallfork, bigfork, napkinknife, spoonglass
Platesmallforkbigforknapkinknifespoonglassplate.

But then one day I made a rainbow
out of Windex and a sunbeam twisting
through the restaurant window.

Now I've done that before
but never noticed, I'm sure.

See before,
making a rainbow
out of invisible
blue cleaner
and a sunbeam
would've been something
tucked away
for childlike eyes
just around the corner
of ordinary, something
I never would've seen,
but today, I found it hovering
there like a patient angel
with a message:
Danny, you're pregnant
with the savior so breathe, breathe.
There's Love in the air.

I have to remember to laugh at myself,
a splashed rain puddle giggle,

because I figure that if I can laugh,
then I'll be okay.
Plus, there's Love in the air–
that Windex rainbow twisting
me out of my ordinary. I'm imagining
a stretch of truth so far that it seems a lie,
a light beam bouncing off these random comet
customers with no aims and turning to moon rays
in the wake of my indigo spray.

Now I'm rough enough to juggle the knuckle
whites of your hand-me-down stress
and I'm tough enough to fit this chaos under my flesh
(yeah, I got thick skin).
I wear order around my collar and sometimes
have to swallow my tongue
just to taste the voice caught in my throat
when I find myself nowhere
in front of your lakeside table–
skipping stones across clarity's gray surface–
and it rises from the seafloor
while it falls from the chandeliers,
and I dip my pen in those very puddles.

I'm not afraid of the hollow and heartless.
Even when they walk through
my section of the restaurant
I'm not afraid. I say,
I've got no compassion
for your future, I'm moving
with the light beams bouncing
off the small things of eternity.
Even if we're all going nowhere
I'm already there
and I feel that God
is the space
between you
and what
you
do.

So, I'm fighting, y'all.

I'm beginning to make dents in this system.
I shovel ice hard like I'm digging a grave for adulthood.
I throw as many plates to the dishwasher as possible—
all the while the beehive swarming itself
into a new sort of trafficked rush hour—
plates I aligned on tables in the first place
like a reincarnation metaphor
my childlike eyes are being reborn
and I'm working the bus station,
waiting for the next customer to come in
and transfer to my route
so I can pick them up a fresh glass of water
without a *thank you*,
but maybe a tip
that smiles when I buy cigarettes.

Plate, small fork, big fork, napkin, knife, spoon, glass, plate.

But I realize that I'm just denting myself
and that's beautiful.
I'm shoveling out that adult now
so after work when the sun's dying
and taking the customers with it,
when I loosen my tie
in order to breathe, breathe,
leaving Windex rainbows crystallized
on the silverware of my memory
and I'm chopping up the old days
with my new soul-buddies,
I can look back and smile laughter
like a splashed rain puddle
as I serve you
these tears in hopes
of quenching the world
with what it needs.

I WILL MEET YOU THERE

–for Irv

Not so long ago now, old friend,
though by foot impossible to reach,
treads the way young poets walk
upon a summer's low-lilting eve.

Beyond the day glade to the elder trees
cloaked in dusk, wandering halcyon,
or away to the languid tavern chatter,
or drawn further yonder by moon ray sent,
the destination is not of matter.

For now, so long ago still reaches
through the low-lilting summer's eve,
where naiad fingers recollect iridescent,
the poet's heart dwelling in eternity.

KNIFE 7

I am considering buying a knife
because I work late hours in a part of town
where people get killed more than I see
or that the news sees, I know it.

Street sweepers were snorting up
the heat-plastered blood from the concrete
when I opened the restaurant this morning.

My hands shook, it felt like shark water.
I may need a knife to protect myself.

I like pyramids, I don't want to
flatline your pyramids.
I don't want to see inside someone like that.
I think every one of your pyramids
happens under its own star.
My daughter wants to go to Egypt
so I've been reading up about it.

My restaurant stays open into the neon.
Henry wanders in then
and we laugh together about nothing
and I make him his midnight omelet.

When he leaves, I hear his harmonica
outside and it sounds better than the devil
could make it sound.
But when the motorized night rumbles
its storm all over our heads,
I hear Henry underwater howl
and it's sad to see an empty hat
and another full bottle.

When Henry leaves,
I think about buying a knife.

I think there are plenty in my kitchen,
but they'll only cut the vegetables
and the prep cook.

My son told me once to imagine
600,000 slot machines
all lined up.
Then he told me to imagine
600,000 people all pulling
the gamble stick
at the same time.

He said, *The chances that all those
machines pull the exact same
images as each other are the same
chances that a human has for even
existing in the universe.*

Then he said, *Dad*, he said,
*Dad, if you lined up 600,000,000
slot machines and repeated the same
experiment with the same results,
that's the chances for this universe to exist.*

Statistics like these make me think
about time and space whenever
I am considering buying a knife.
I make the knife a big picture.

30 knives are purchased a week
in my neighborhood, so says
the smoke shop owner.
3 out of those 30 get used
to confiscate time and space
from someone's body, he reasons.

I am in a place where I have to make my own
statistics to cheer up sometimes.

1 out of every 2 people will fall in love.
The other half must not want to.

If 108 people fall in love this week
in my neighborhood,
that'll be 54 new couples.
If a third of them are vegetarians,

then 36 new people will find their way
into my restaurant for romance without meat.

That means I need to buy
18 new beautiful red candles.

CHAPTER III
MYTHOS

THE BELLMAKER OF SANJESKA DEZELA

At some distance, the poet watched while the villagers of Sanjeska Dezela disassembled his body. He observed them discover how the intricate bone structure of his writing hand was not composed of bone at all but of windchimes.

The poet overheard the villagers arrive at the consensus that this meant he was born with a natural ability for dancing in the wind.

Curious about the poet's travels, the villagers then set to work opening his feet. They found his oaken toes gigantic and finger-like, his wizened soles impenetrable. They scraped away with the blade of a conch shell, but doing so seemed only to induce the effect of polishing fine wood, and, try as they might, they could not separate callous from flesh.

The villagers determined the poet must have once walked barefoot on the moon and the seafloor alike, and they left it at that.

The villagers then untangled the poet's calves, pulling apart the tendons like so much bramble, and when they did so, the waters of many rivers began to flow forth from the estuaries. The village cartographer discerned three rivers out of the multitude: Tigris, Oceanus, and Gjöll. There existed, the cartographer disclosed, hidden rivers—their names retained solely in fox lore—their pronunciation invoked by the wavering syllables of mist.

And far away, the Bellmaker began to work.

The kneecaps were both uncorked. One's edge perfected the craft of canoe carving; the other became a receptacle for the pyramidal bricks of ash tapped from the glowing ends of the renowned cigars of Sanjeska Dezela.

The poet watched the amputation of his scrotum and member. The scrotum, once hollowed, swiftly became a handbag—the style of which was fashionable in the Younger Dryas. The member, a kind of prismatic stalagmite, was severed from its foundation and laid horizontally into the womb of a wooden ark. The villagers cast the makeshift ark upon the opaline sea, and, seemingly by its own volition, it steered itself toward the heliacal rise of the star of Aphrodite.

A gaunt hand plunged a volcanic and sawtooth blade between
the clavicles. The blade torqued downwards, its point striking an
extraterrestrial stone. As the blade wedged through the solar plexus, the
chest creaked like bamboo bending or like the slow croak of a raven.
Then, the palms of the rib cage opened wide, their insides tasting, for
the first time, the vision of the moon along her skyward path. The
point of that blade, scraping across the contours of the depths, sent an
indecipherable cursive of meteorite sparks through their midst. Upon
removal, the villagers saw the blade dwindling into nothingness. The
poet's heart remained unscathed, for it dwelt elsewhere, beyond the hoary
oasis of Sanjeska Dezela.

And meanwhile, the Bellmaker was fast at work.

As if to catch rainwater leaking from a shanty roof, the villagers set clay
jars below the poet's body wherever his darkling blood did drip. His lips
illumined with the memory of deep Syrian wine and seraph song alike,
opened just so at the approach of a veiled goddess. With a fey forefinger,
she placed a singular teardrop upon them. The sinewy muscles of the
poet's entire body relaxed, his blood deluging each clay jar to the brim.
Then, the goddess departed, a shadow of cloud indistinguishable from the
night.

Once uprooted from its den, the tongue possessed the peculiar effect
of setting ablaze all who dared hold it. By relay from one brave runner
to the next, the poet's tongue flew to roost in a new mouth–that of a
labyrinthine cave in which the catacombs of Sanjeska Dezela were hewn.
Even now, on auspicious days, light refracts into this labyrinth, splashing
its spectral asterisms to dance far into the depths.

The elegant and gibbous trigon of the poet's nose transformed into a
cherry blossom in the palm of a hunter.

A child drew near and twirled a finger into the temple of the poet's skull,
then backed away, giggling at the sky-blue paint that began to soak his
hand.

They opened the left eyelid, unleashing a banshee whose howl sent the
masses reeling. After she went whipping away, the crowd composed
themselves and cautiously opened the right eyelid. One by one, the
villagers took turns peering into this meadow-wed fane, a place long
forgotten in the broken echo of a dream.

The poet looked on as the villagers detached each of his eyes. As was their custom, they placed a wildflower in both chasms after doing so. The eyes went to the high priestess, who passed a thumb across each iris.

Death and Life, she said, *are so close as to be one.*

The Bellmaker's work was almost complete as the veiled goddess fastened the last bell into its place.

Those who peered into the poet's ears heard a faint voice in their chests. The voice forged images of stories in their hearts, impossible and clear. The voice, they agreed later, felt like hope.

Now, as the child used the paint found in the temple of the poet to make rainbows occur on the stone steps of Sanjeska Dezela that descend to the shore, an ancient woman shook his spine like a rain-stick or a spear.

The poet's skin started to resemble quicksand.

A wind rumor spiraled above the village, then gusted low, soaring through the empty corridors.

The poet began to dance his invisible dance.

The villagers of Sanjeska Dezela realized a storm was brewing and began to seek shelter while ravens took into the sky what remained of the poet's carcass.

From inside their dusky homes, the villagers heard thunder paralyze time with each strike. Lightning bursts revealed their shrewd faces to each other. The limbs of the rain beast went drumming through the streets— its river tides knocking over the clay jars filled with the blood of the poet—and the two liquids swept into one another, the blood and the rain, making an elixir drunk between the cobbled stones.

The wind grew tranquil and wandered away, and the rain beast stampeded into the distance beyond the hills. Thunder and lightning bowed and took their leave as the poet's dance drew to a close.

The solemn hearths of Sanjeska Dezela kindled in their quietude as the villagers drifted into dreamless sleeps.

Lucid stars plotted themselves upon the horizon once the clouds unraveled about the wake of the moon.

Somewhere, tornado dust settled on a wave in the shape of the poet's thumbprint.

Far away, the Bellmaker rested below the frost-glistened boughs.

GILGAMESH

O Hero,
I inversed your myth,
I bifurcated it.

I measured
your stellar catharsis
from Uruk through Wadlyng Street.

You, warrior turned astronomer
you, antediluvian refugee,
perhaps you silenced,
for a moment centuries long,
the schizophrenia of the gods.

I know not
if you and I are alike
(you: Force
and we think ourselves
Necessity).
Though, perhaps,
we once corresponded
on Alpha Carinae.

When you returned to Iraq in the end
with a star called Urshanabi
you bade him measure your city
as the reader is asked to at the start.

I, stellified, grasped your walls of Uruk then,
for they compose the very words of your tale.

Gilgamesh, my people no longer slay gods,
the sky lost, celestial motions crumbling
into obliquity, into the undecipherable.

Yet, the walls of Uruk endure, Hero-
walls translated into verse
verse translated into a hidden architecture
irrefragable and infinite,
beyond our ability to rupture.

FROM A NEW RENDERING OF GILGAMESH

TABLET IX

Gilgamesh entered the wilderness
in bitter mourning. Sorrow possessed his heart
as he journeyed, weeping for his friend.
He went wondering if death would come to him
in the same manner through the darkness.
In the wake of a dream, an ancient name
voyaged to him on his memory.
The name of a man who, in watercraft,
was vouchsafed from death long ago, then
made immortal in distant lands. Utnapishtim
was his name, the Faraway: Hero of the Flood.
Utnapishtim, who, immortal, knew
the secrets of the gods and the world before
the Deluge. Gilgamesh resolved to seek,
despite great peril, his ancestor,
distant Utnapishtim, the Faraway.
For in its tearful midst, his heart desired
above all, to learn the mystery
of existence, to discover if death
can be escaped by one such as himself.

★★★

Still, despair possessed him in the roaming gloom.
In the gloaming doom, in a mountain pass
surrounded by danger, terror seized him.
Gilgamesh prayed in moon rays invisible, and
by this lamp, the light of the Lady of the gods
poured down, courage-kindling
the gladness of life in Gilgamesh's heart.
He drew his adz, falling upon his assailants,
the nocturnal beasts, scattering them like splinters
of bright meteor dust smote across the night sky.

His body became hair-covered and hirsute

as he wandered bitter-weeping through mist-woven
dayscapes indistinguishable from nightscapes.
The wild's skin donned Gilgamesh limb by limb.
His prey-food became the beasts that stalked him.
In mountainsides, he dug wells, finding water
hidden, and he chased the wanton winds alone
until he arrived at this interval's end,
Mount Mashu, whose summit lifts the cloth
of the celestial firmament, whose roots
ensnare the Underworld in their grasp,
and the vanishing sun does travel
at times through the center of.

★★★

Twin Scorpions guard the gate at Mount Mashu
with the radiance of Antares,
their countenance celestial and terrible
to witness. The darkness of Mashu is dazzled
with *melammu*–the aura of they, who,
keeping their watch over the sun's path,
are known to us by the name *Scorpius*.

At the threshold, Gilgamesh summoned
great courage, conjuring together his wits.
He approached with reverence the Scorpion
Being whose colossal Constellation
towers forever in the heavens.

God flesh this man grows, spoke the male Scorpion.
The female Scorpion Twin replied,
Two-thirds is god. One-third is but mortal.

The Scorpion Being addressed Gilgamesh
and said, *You draw near the confluence
of rivers. Why? How did you journey here?*

In awe, Gilgamesh responded, *I seek
the path my forefather faired. Utnapishtim,
who was made eternal by the gods.
I seek from him the secret of death and of life.*

The Scorpion Being responded and said,
Never before has a mortal passed through Mashu,
where light itself dares not travel, knowing
not dawn gleam nor gloaming shimmer nor sunrise
ray or sunset glimmer; where there is darkness
upon darkness twelve leagues dense; where around
the mouth of this passageway light itself bends.

Gilgamesh listened to these words and said,
I know this frostbitten, bitter, windswept road
has been my road. Sorrow-torn, mourning,
sojourning the wild alone, I found my way
here despite it and I shall prevail through
despair and exhaustion. Now open
the gate for Gilgamesh, the king of Uruk!

The Scorpion Being spoke and said, *Go then*
King Gilgamesh! May Mount Mashu allow
you to pass through her womb unharmed.
May the ranging darkness permit you to traverse
with ease. May you journey with steady foot
the darkness ahead. The mountain has
now opened her gates before you, Gilgamesh!

The words of the Scorpion Being
spirited Gilgamesh, and he began
following the path forward through darkness.

ʌ ʌ ʌ

At the first league, darkness enveloped him.
The Scorpion Twin's shimmer was already gone.

At the second league, the darkness was quite deep.
His body vanished, became shadow.

At the third league, the darkness intensified.
There was no shadowhand before his face.

At the fourth league, darkness compacted, absorbing all.
Light itself became difficult to remember.

At the fifth league, the roots of darkness plunged deeper.
The memory of light dissolved, abandoning him.

At the sixth league, he tried to speak: *Twin companions strive
as one…* But his words hid themselves away in his heart.

At the seventh league, even his footsteps vanished
becoming shapeless shades in a void.

At the eighth league, he began a soundless sprint.

At nine leagues, he felt the fingertips of Tumumir,
the North Wind, stray across his face.
Still, no light shone in the formless cave.

At the tenth league, the darkness seemed the density of the second.
He knew not that he drew near the end.

At the eleventh league, he had the journey
of one to go (though he knew it not),
the shadow of Shamash lay cast across him.

After twelve leagues he emerged,
heralding the dawn when sunrise erupted,
scattering itself hematite-like across
the surface of the distant, almost unseen sea.

★★★

By dawn glow, cosmic greenery, and jungle-like,
the foliage rose, radiating vines
along granite-high mountainsides into cloud
forests aloft, their altitudes invisible
through divine vapor sent down before him.
Moss made pathways wound around
mist-hewn rock shapes. He ambled
an easeful descent, soothing dew-blue
droplets upon his tor-worn feet.
Disbelief he harbored, yet with gentle fingers
he glanced a small carob shrub whose fog-rippled
branches bent just so while before him lingered
wild glades swayed in dawn hue, their jade boughs

amethyst drenched by the aquatic light
moving within the cypress-stemmed and cedar
seeded eternities, alive, where stood
lapis lazuli-fruit flourishing trees
unaware of thirst: the forms of forests known
these designs birthed.
Then, a happenstance wildflower path
winding thither along. Blades of touch-grass sprouting
from fertile earth elapsing on whim
spaced themselves between his footsteps, adorned
by petals of asterisms swirling,
drooping, precessing; a lilting, lush road
rivering onto copses blossoming
in mystical depths where secret spirit rites
must occur. He observed the stellar serenade,
drawn into each flora-vein visible
and a'pulse with pure lifeblood quenching root,
trunkstem, to the end of each thistle-burst.
Forest fronds wind-bow, their living carnelian
green leaves exist somehow humble in their drowning,
indomitable vitality.
Incandescent beyond measure. Luminosity
blooming, a celestial organism
whose canopy verses star lore. Thornless.
A galaxy of spontaneity
flowing pristine. Lullaby of meadowmist,
primal dwelling place of Rain where Fire sleeps
beneath the hearth of Rest. Indigo, gray,
emerald-black, from sapphire etched,
entwined, harmonizing petal-colors
ever branching beneath the fragrant breath of sky.
This oasis of dreaming paradise-rooted
and boundless, planted prismatic in
each star woven, wind-drenched, and rain-sent
atom. This garden meadows then wetlands,
ponds mirror, willows wisp, then wetlands meadow
again weaving onto a shore savanna-like.
Sea waves roll along coral calling,
clanging, the chiming ocean over sasu-stone
and abashmu-rock. Vertical roots echo
the rustling forest shivers windward
with presence. Before him, the sea unfolds, vast

and shimmering. Horizons wreathed in unique
majesty. Eternal vision strays where
wanderer cannot stay. Heartbroken
king, from bitter wilderness to space dark cave,
sidereal wayfarer through fey forest glade
now walked, as a visitor in a dream,
along the edge of the sun-carved sea.

And from the stoep of her tavern-inn
veiled Siduri observed him draw near.

WE ARE PROMETHEUS

I

All religions are one
The voice of one crying in the wilderness.

–William Blake

II

Sufi poetry has been used
to liberate the Islamic peoples
for centuries.
It has also been used as war poetry
for Jihad.

Hafiz, a Sufi Poet says,
I am a hole in a flute
that the Christ's breath moves through.
Listen to this music.

It is said that Jesus was sacrificed
to save us from our sins.
God then did
what Abraham did not.

III

Would you allow yourself to be
crucified on a sawed-off dream?
Is your body holy land?
If so, it is our bodies that are
our common ground.
Is it the same blood that flows
throughout your entire body?
If you saw God's blood spilt
across your body, would you believe then?

IV

Do the prisoners in Guantanamo

feel like they are on Mars?
How could such a thing exist on Earth?
How could we let it?

V

Does your heart
sometimes feel
as far away
as Mars?

Is there a Guantanamo in your heart?
Are you holding anyone prisoner in those chambers?

Guns have chambers too.
How many bullets should we load
into your heart's chambers?
I will spin them like a shrapnel cyclone
and we'll both play Russian Roulette.

VI

Who is controlling you?
Is your right arm controlled by your brain?
(Even as you cast prayers
into the supple sand
waves then vanish.)
Is your right arm Israeli?

Is your mind the US?

And those river stones you carry
tucked under your left arm,
the ones that you would hurl
into giants and humvees and tanks,
did you find them in a Palestinian river?
Is your left arm Palestine?
Are you playing bloody knuckles with yourself?

VII

Is it because your mind is telling you to?

Or have you lost your mind?
Your heart should make your mind function.

Your heart beating life
through your veins,
blood kept prisoner
by your veins,
do you need to set it free?
Do you need to set Life free, soldier?

VIII

I believe hearts can kill people
it's just that spades usually do first,
Holy Roller,
the sky's poker face isn't fooling me
though, I didn't know your heart
was big enough to contain Mars,
I see it now shimmering in the distance
like a bullet coming at me in time lapse.

IX

Mars is made of metal and space fire
sparks. His eyes frosted bloodshot,
his hands outstretched like eagle talons,
he is reaching for my mortality.

X

Are we praying to the wrong God?
Are we praying to Mars?
Don't fight wars with your heart.
Still your hand with it. Let it see
the merciful angels and rams tangled
in thorns. Steal fire with it, for my palms
enkindle heat more brilliant than Mars.

XI

Prometheus, I will take your place on the cliff.
I invite the beaks of eagles to rip me open,

for tied inside this body I cannot always do it myself.
Descend conduit eagles. Let my spirit hemorrhage
through the palms of my wounds, pumping pulse
like volume, I will drench their feather tips heavy
with my blood until they cannot lift away.

And scraping their wings
across the cliff side
they will compose
the story of us all.

URSHANABI

The Inkling tells me
to describe it like this:
I've got a new employer.

I work for the Myth now, my friend.
I speak island verse with urnu-snakes
and listen to fox-lore with sorceresses
in starry forests when rain meadow makes.

I won't try to convince you, though,
of the reality of naiad sooth
or discuss in-depth the morphology
of wood duck jargon.

What you up to these days? they ask.

I'm just the riverman in the wide hat.
On a mist-hewn August morning
sometimes I drift around the bend.

CHAPTER IV
LOVE AS LIGHTNING

SHADES OF ORANGE

It's so hot, my armpits are flowing
fountains forth of the drinks
I've not stopped quaffing
since happy hour first flowered
and the fountains
are turning the chalices
vermillion of my coral-colored shirt—
my *shirt* since this is the sort of establishment
in which a shirt indeed is worn—
and you decide to perch
next to me at the sparse expansive bar
with your flashy
black fingernails
and your pointy, pointy boots
and these two effects
emblazing you, svelte and elfin,
spelled Trouble
so, I asked if you wanted
to share an orange with me.

I'd love to, you said.
But oranges are not on the menu…

Bartender! I hailed.
An orange, please.

And he took one out
of his secret bartending bowl
and he tossed it to me
and I *caught* it
(which is rare)
and my coolness culminated
when I handed you the orange
and said, *Peel it.*

Now, peeling an orange can be sticky business
and I'm pretty sure that tight scarlet-striped shirt
you're wearing cost more than my wardrobe,
but you must have fingers like Ferraris darlin'
'cause we started mawin' down on orange sections

faster than most celebrities get caught shoplifting.

And you did sorta steal my heart when between
a fresh slice of citrus town and guzzling down
your fourth cosmopolitan you asked me,
So, how many kids know you're their dad, anyways?

But I didn't answer because
I noticed stage left where
I thought I saw a tiny human
plucking, on an incredibly large
fulvous guitar,
an acoustic cover of "Exit"
by Tangerine Dream,
and pointed the situation out to you,
and watched your foxlike eyes narrow
as you leaned in and said,
Danny, that is a normal-sized person
playing a standup bass.
The song's "You're Always On Time"
but you're aces for naming the band, mate.

I hope your hair smells like spaghetti, I said.
I want my hair to smell like you, you said.
No, I said in the heatwave gloam. *You don't.*

We stumbled off into the August eve
like two toppling dreidels,
we freak danced
to the bassline dropped thick
by the passing cars,
we went too far in public
amidst the bioluminescent air,
blah blah blah…

I think the reason I wrote this to you
is to say that night
our tongues
were like mermaids,
and our bodies
were like mermaid magnets.
I know how so many parts of you taste

and they all taste like oranges–
that thing you said
was not on the menu.

URSA MAJOR

1

You are wearing my blue beanie
like a gang sign
you move like you know one day
you will have three wooden fingers
and a peg leg
but a spine you could sharpen
diamonds on

2

Imagining a rickety old you
with a caryatid skeleton
laughing like witchcraft
and using the weathervanes
to show tourists the direction
heaven is

3

Kleptomaniacs
shoplifting our breath
from the top shelves of one another

4

The one who draws me
Imaginista
the reason I ever returned

5

Away from you
I remember
the journal you gave me
is the same size as my passport

6

Through your eyes
the song of a torn cloud
weaves me
while your name is a constellation
glinting like the stars between my teeth
I sing your name glinting
through this abyss
at which we still joyously laugh

7

Last night I realized all that
we have in common
how we bear the same foible
we are free

FRAGMENT FROM THE TIME I LIVED NEAR THE MOON

These are the days I want Velocity to take me,
unglue my soul from its fish tank.
I know how to breathe in outer space,
I kiss with three eyes open,
I see the ice sickle in your Romantic,
I'm asking my cataclysm to resuscitate itself:
I don't want to walk through the dark
with a single candle lit.
Watch,
I will begin to bleed starlight
from my palms. I have enough fire
to keep Day around until tomorrow.
I've gotten so high since you left
that I've considered sharpening my thoughts
until they could rip through the space/time continuum
and I could sort of slip over
the edge of the universe
as if the universe were a pupil and I
were a teardrop, and I wonder if the universe
would catch me in Her hands,
lift me up the way grown men still want their fathers
to lift them up
sometimes, and put me back
or I wonder if She would just let me fall
to Her feet twirling around a pole
like a beautiful stripper
shedding Her clothes like light. Spreading
open all the minds of the men around like legs.
All it takes is just one apple
to penetrate revelation,
        Does She cry for you? Is She perpetually
        falling for you?
        Does Her weight give
        you scoliosis in the backbone, your need-bones
        trembling slacked down on the heart's hips,
        Body, can you walk, straight up?

Look: She's dressed in waves now.

She's blowing you kisses that could drown
you. They could pull you in, cast you
3,000 miles away. You know not
what it feels like to be shipwrecked
in the city of dreams where She wears
clothes made of concrete so tight
Her body bleeds starlight
onto rivers parted like lovers
by bra strap bridges
that keep transportation
pressed together. The wrists of Her sky
always scraped. Sing Her body electric.
The holes we burrowed into
Her arm and Her big toe, running
across these tracks, you will never find Her heart.

Be not afraid of Her.
Her body tremoring beneath her blanket—
earthquakes of the spirit or subway trains
on fire, whatever way you choose to see it.

Look: Her skin glistens like sweat or twilight.
She does not reach up to you for change.
She reaches up to the moon
glowing blue behind you,
drifting, She says, *Lift me up
the way you once did.*

And you know
She is
just talking
to Herself.

CHERRY BLOSSOM

The last time I got turned inside
   out I recognized myself
   I am someone who has learned
   to nurse the scars within

I know I can get carried away
   like a baby in a basket on a river
or a riot sometimes
   you see me in two places
 at once just sitting over there

Look at my eyes
   they are head-on collisions
my eyes are the ripple
   in your stomach
when you wish
   you were dreaming
my eyes are distanced
   they turn my hometown to dust cloud
and mangled strips of speed limit
   my eyes are burning rubber
all that I will show you are my eyes
   they are license plates,
random configurations
of letters and numbers
   that tell you absolutely
nothing about who I really am
my heart is what God can do
   with a single teardrop
   my heart is a river winding
   through outer space
and I am looking for my riverbed
   I am looking
for my riverbed
   Moses show me my riverbed

I am looking to be reminded
that I am something more than water
   so the next person to dip
their hand into my chest

can memorize the way out
by the map of scars
   written on my walls
like cave paintings

TOUCH

Every time the muse dreams me
I'm left as thirsty as a man
just made out of the dust itself.

I spill my guts like a tidal wave
and see who is left on the shore
when the tide goes back out.

My blood says that it's my water
dancing like a chimp in my veins.
Go ahead, my blood jests, *cut deep,*
pour me down your throat. You still
won't have any idea who you are.

I dig into my womb
and carve chunks of spirit-charge
into symbols that prove how impossible
I am, how superhuman I can be.
I want love to be as honest
as dying, as human
as dying. I want love to be water
spilled across the grease fire fist
of a brain punching doubt-bricks.

Love, they told me,
will fill everything with light.

On the bus,
I talk to my phone
with nobody in a language
I make up on the spot.
People look at me differently;
I feel like I'm being myself.
I ask for directions I will never follow
and pretend to know where I am
in this heart-wave,
I dip my bare feet in hope
and walk down writer's block.
I plunge my palms in guilt
and do handstands in front

of the courthouse on Sundays.
By Monday, all my stories
are washed away.

In this town,
longing and home
share one location–
a word that fits in my heart
heavy like an anchor.
I drop it on this gray street.

Tonight, I will dream here
rolling a thorn between my lips.

I have learned how to draw blood
so now my inside touches everything.
It doesn't always turn to gold.

MERCY

Agni, I never wrote about you
before. Your perfume curls my hair.
You caught my shadow light
upon your stare. You, you ruined my life.
You made me homeless. With no knife,
I wandered alleyways
and strange forgotten places,
all those places & the people walking by,
I saw you like a cloud
passing over their faces.

You lost me
in Eichstätt, Querétaro, New York City.
Eichstätt, it is in a valley
that becomes filled with mist,
and during an old war
was hidden from the soldiers
because the mist had filled it.

This is the condition you leave me in, Agni:
sunken, missed, and lonely.
My name should really be Atlantis,
for I howl with the mermaids
and know each of their dances.
Their earrings worn on another lover's ear–
antiques I pawned in old markets
by the sea or underneath
freeway bridges. Agni, forgive me. I tried
pawning pieces of you to get them back.

This exquisite blur you wrapped around me,
one moment I am in Lima,
the next, Poznań, the next, Montréal
and nowhere I fit in,
a foxhole buried in a telescope, I don't fit in.

I am writing this on paper I found in the trash.
It's cold, 10 pm, and I only ate once.

Agni, my chipped tooth is aching,

there's still a few smokes left to
my name. Not from this world. I don't fit in.

I am a sideways beam of
light stumbling drunken
down the street.

There is a flower in my hand.
I do not know if it is
love I feel or you, or You.
In my hand there is a flower.
I took up smoking just to deal with you.
Smoke blossoms from my fingers.

Agni, I am grateful it was you who ruined my life
and not someone I mistook for you,
wielder of the Ziggurat, the Fire, and the Night.

AMARANTHINE

I see you,
October on your fingertips,
plucking a banshee-chord in the empty courtyard,
cigarette lit between your lips.
You look like a folktale
with that guitar whirling
motion in your arms.
Your petals nightingale-rippling in waves of wind
evening-drenched, star-riddled, chanting
your mountainous immensity,
your meadow-wed unmanifested fane,
darkling blossom upon river droplets,
Sorceress in the rain.
You, the dream that awakens,
dissolve me into embers amethyst and sheer,
indistinguishable from the night. Vibrant
in your daybreak cocoon
as in the dawn sky when we find the moon.
And while your song vanishes
slow beyond the earth, after all
you set in motion passes away
finds itself, through your magic, rebirthed.

CHAPTER V
NOSTOS

POINT B

A whole lot of attention's paid to the way
one gets from Point A to Point B.
Now, I've never seen Point B for real.
I'm not even positive it exists.

I'm a humble representative from Point A.
In my time, I visited Points E, L, and W.
(I flew over G once and found it opalescent, sonorous.)

Although I'm simply a representative,
I feel that these Points have met.
They've mingled, the Points, they made ends meet.
Or, perhaps, I assisted in the gathering of Points
merely by meandering all over the map.

What am I getting to?

Well, some friends of mine
who act like they live in Point B
harbor some opinions:
You've got your fists up, they say.
You need to scrap that chain mail.

And I remind them that opinions
are just imaginary friends for adults
(and this here, my friend,
is my imaginary friend).

And they say, *Okay, so my imaginary friend
is saying to you that you should question
your invincibility every now and then.*

I'm much better at listening
to my friend's imaginary
friends than their opinions.
So, I looked at the suit of armor I assembled
over here in Point A
and figured that it maybe was fueled
by deep-seated superstitions,
some paranoia surrounding an archaic curse

that I required the *Lance of Liquorouage*
to protect myself from,
and that nihilistic, smoke-riddled breastplate
which, steadfast nonetheless,
seemed only to leave me out of breath.

Although most people in Point B
hold little to no belief in magic,
a friend of mine rumored to live there
once whispered to me
the danger of losing what little I still possessed
if I kept wearing the armor.
But by now, the armor already punctured my flesh
and seeped around my bones.

How do I shed the armor? I begged my beloved friend.

By waking up a little earlier,
by coming home a little earlier.
Let vegetables find a sacred place in your heart.
Get your green thumbs out of your ass,
it's been spring for months for fuck's sake!

This advice left me understood.
And understanding, I began to investigate.

I didn't go by the book. At first
the clues felt like mistakes I made,
but I followed them nonetheless.

I jangled a few petty locks,
roughed up a minotaur or two
for clues in the labyrinths
behind those locks. Learned
I'd need to travel back through time.

I hopped a train to the cloud forests of Point T
around which the sun neither rises nor sets.

Then a ship to Point M
to make amends to a sorceress
disguised as a dancer in a moon blue dress.

After we spoke, she drew me
a card that read, *Surrender.*

The semblance of a picture began to emerge.

Along my way, I rescued a wolf cub in Q,
landlocked and lonesome,
where an ancient aqueduct
crumbles into the dawn.

I'd gotten married in Point Z,
where my wife almost killed me
trying to rip the breastplate off
but that was lifetimes ago
before the war in X
where I'd lost the lance and my way
wandering back through the fatigued
world that then seemed so pointless.

I remember the feeling,
like being trapped
on the floating islands of L.
The constellations kept breaking
up and rearranging like an amoeba
my touchstones were not anchored…
my witnesses were nowhere to be found…

Then, one dawn, I wrote some words
in the sand on the shore
and the waves took them away
as if the waves were translating
what I'd written into *Ocean*
and for a moment I thought I saw
Point B rising out of the sea,
but deep down I knew I'd never left
Point A. Not really.

What am I getting to,
all armor-less and naked as a baby bobcat?

Well, I've got some friends, really good friends,
who wouldn't be able to understand all these points

because they haven't explored them.
But these friends, they worry about me so much
I can't even believe it sometimes.

The thing, they say, *about living in Point A,*
is that there you don't care about anything or anyone.
You just let everyone else do all the caring.

But I'm beginning to understand that.

That is like resolving to stay
inside of a prison
without a lock
on a single door.

SERAPHIM

One day, I'll tell you the story of how I talked to Fire
and changed.
Not at this point. One day.
No, perhaps I will never tell you!
The sweet secret of it, what Fire said.
If you offended your Star
so She turned her back on you
causing your life to go to shame
and bringing you to ruin.
One day, I will tell you what Fire said.
One day, I'll reveal to you how to get Her back.
You see, the tears and the shaking must come first.
You must be tortured but not ready to give in.
If you manage between the gasps to speak
some true words from your heart
or the place where your heart once was
the ash-riddled chasm
a tree dared grow from.
If the rain is falling, but the birds know what to do.
If She turns to you and moves a little closer,
you might still be in the doghouse,
but at least it is Her doghouse.
Fire will speak to you, break you, open you
lay your body down, teach you to stand up
from where your body lays, flicker & change,
if you can grow while dissolving into Her flames,
then Fire, with wise-cracking know-how,
might impart some words of wisdom on you.

A SONG FOR AUTUMN

Before the sinews of your leaves released their grip
the riverbed opened wide her ancient palms
and we read of rest in their braided lines.
Then, up above, the wind-made paths of cobblestone clouds
wandered slow, bearing their harvest to the hearth of sky.

Before all your leaves made light their burden
your limbs were wizened with the wisdom
of abundance, humbled with bowing
under the weight of wings.
You who are tree-versed in this ritual of falling,
this vessel of release: enter the hearth of rest.
Your bark star-saturated and hailstorm-strong
your roots travel deeper than frost can reach.

Before the sinews of your leaves released their grip
they blazed. Each held their torch aloft
designating you our steadfast guide
beyond solstice. Transmigrating through the unknown–
the revelatory unknowing–
that always seems to be cradled as it crumbles,
dreaming into the womb of Life.

THE BOAT CARVER

The woman at the deli
of the supermarket commented,
You look like you've had a long day.

The word *work* spelled between
her wrinkles in two languages
at once. I'm pale and embarrassed.

A joke got caught
on the clothes hanger
in my throat.
All I said was, *Yeah.*

She's three times older than me,
laughs like she knows what I was
going to say, and hands me my lunch.

I smell the food my work
paid for and find it in me
to unbutton my voice and ask,
How do you do it?

Her wrinkles rise,
erase *work*,
and rewrite *joy*.

I have four kids, she says.
*Two of them are at the age
where they need cell phones.
I pay for their communication.
I used to make bridges from
English to my feelings, but no
one could cross them, except
for my husband (see, he speaks
my language).*

*There is an island
you can only get to by boat.
Noah found it, you know.*

We are all islands, dear,
every one of us.
And I carve boats
from the trees
my parents worked for.

And I work.
To know where my children are,
and to help them along the way
to where they are going.

DISTANCE

Put me in the Distance.

Now, if you've never heard
of the Distance, it's out there.
It's sort of like where the Truth has this way
of answering all your questions
without even having to speak,
like the first time you set eyes
on the First Love of your life
as they were just walking down the street.

Put me in the Distance
where you can riddle rumors
out about my existence.
Perhaps someone might say,
I heard that Danny vanished,
but every now and then
I catch a word from a bird
that he made it far away,
some place shaped by a wave,
and started carving boats
in a meadow maker's glade.

See, when I'm in the Distance,
Mythmaking—
it won't be my job anymore,
it'll be yours,
and I think it would be just what the doctor ordered
if I were in the Distance so long
that there was a band of Danny impersonators
running the alleyways of the world
like quicksand horses
that everyone's eyes could sort of sink into.

And I feel it, like our hearts
are all in the Distance pumping
Vision into our blood and blood
back into our vision. Distance is
being able to see things from
the inside out. Distance is where

the future grows. Distance puts
the marrow in Tomorrow. Distance
is what I wanna eat for breakfast,
it's the bull's eye tattooed to the inside
of my solar plexus and only the Sunset
can pierce it. So, when I'm gone,

I'll be gone.
My back will be turned
by the time your arrows are drawn
and the Distance that I'm all wrapped up in
will put the potential energy in your quiver.

Distance is the backbone in my swagger
and the twang in my stupid honesty.

See, without the Distance,
my gunslinger's wrists
hang lifeless with arthritis at my sides
and the wanderer of my lips
forgets how to kiss the sky.
Without the Distance, some nights,
I grind my wisdom teeth into a fine powder
and I lace my cigarettes with it.
Other nights, I use it to fill the empty hour glasses.
I put them in the world where things always
get turned upside down and
to feel like I have more time,
I do headstands on escalators.

I'll hit my spirit with a reflex hammer
just to see if its knee jerks,
I'll get used to the different-day-same-t-shirt.
I'll play with symbols in reverse and reverse
till I bleed Earth. Listen, these words
are patchwork nothing. I left my patchworks
right between West 4th and Bleecker.

Now I bare knuckle box the past
with a blindfold on. I keep Tomorrow
a breath away, and break dawn
like an egg across the home of your hate.

Because Distance
is a dynamite sack of static
packed with matchsticks stuck on motion
and I am a river stone explosion,
a chiseled whisper,
an echo crumbling into itself,
a clover growing its fourth leaf:
CheckYourKineticsCheckMyKinetics
striking lightning off the brail of our pulse.

Put me in the Distance and I will go.

I will go to the Pawnshop at the End of the Universe
where the pawnshop owner keeps his beard in check
with that razor blade you may have traded in for a second chance.
And he'll look at me from behind those elusive crossed arms
and that wayward smile pawnshop owners often have,
and I'll just take a look around. I'll see the angel wings slung
up on the walls and all of our old dreams bottled in jars on shelves
that slant for the weight, until I realize that this is as far as I can go.

I'll move the Distance
out of the way,
walk up to that pawnshop owner
and say, *Listen,*
I've got a great story.
It's about a spirit
trying to find his way back to his bones.
And I'm willing to trade it in
just so long as you can give me directions
on how to get back home.

RAINDROP

Born from the chaos of the storm,
your iridescence rippled with knowing
the center of the flame.

Pull your hands now from the center of the flame
and descend from the treacherous heavens
for your heart awaits you
in the silence of the Earth.

She, the hidden music of morning,
waits to draw your song into her lucidity.

Now, together, unfold yourselves into the dawn
and let the stars open wide their windows
so your melody may fill their homes.

Sprites of the wine-dark sea,
invite weary wanderers through your door.
Quench those who thirst with a wave.
Weave your terrestrial syzygy from the invisible
and paint it around our bones.

O little raindrop,
who carves planets from the vastness,
who with a flood sets life ablaze,
you, in whose hands shall be placed to mend
those fragments of sky when it shatters.

THE EXQUISITE DARK

For still the names on the gravestones.

Let the stone-cutter work renderings
of my palms into the epitaph.
For this way the meaning
would dwell in the place
where your fingers fit into mine.

Let the palm readers come describe
destiny there in the cemetery
and to its silent steadfastness-
the prehistoric signature, the torchlit
handprint extinguished from sight.

For though stone fingers cannot interlock
with your own, they beckon you to imagine.

Imagine.

Let all you might hold elevate
the living in the handful of syllables
given you to toil miracles with.

For the architects,
and we, scrappers,
for the translators,
for we charm.

ACKNOWLEDGEMENTS

My deepest gratitude radiates to everyone who fostered a love for words within me. From the poets of old (whose names now are remembered and lost) to my family who placed books in my hands as soon as I could hold them, I thank you for blessing me with this gift and reverence for language. I thank my parents for often reading and singing me to sleep. To my brother, thank you for reading me Tolkien, and introducing me to the Tao. To my sister, thank you for introducing me to the most ancient of epics.

I am greatly indebted to the mentors of my youth: El Día, Roberto Ascalon, Tara Hardy, Rajnii Eddins, Jojo Gaon, Jack McCarthy, and Karen Finneyfrock. You taught me to see the spirit in the words and how to become that spirit. With humility and honor, I call myself your student. I hope to return what you granted me by sharing it with those authors and storytellers in whose midst I have the luck of finding myself.

My astonishment at the timely magic with which Write Bloody approached me to re-release this collection persists. I remain in awe of Derrick Brown's impeccable eye and ability to see hidden themes in the texts. I am indebted to Haley Hutchinson for catching more than a few editorial calamities before it was too late. It is a deep joy to revisit these poems and continue to metamorphose through this process.

I am blessed each day by a community of islanders with whom I share a spiritual practice. Without your influence, I would not still be here. I'm overjoyed to trudge (while blossoming an indefatigable faith in Love) beside you on this Road. My most Salish Seawave-woven and madrona-riddled thanks to the Island Verse crew. You inspire me and make me giggle, shiver, and focus. I'm ecstatic about the wonder we craft. I give great thanks to Nate Fihn for your indomitable heart, your warm sense of community, your keen discernment, and your mesmerizing wordmagic. I likewise offer profound gratefulness to Maria Michaelson for your quirky and majestic wisdom, the weariless fire of your creativity, and your dazzling spirit. Thank you for the transcendent collaboration, the dance-spangled journey, the secret passages into the myth, and the courage to know the real span of my wings.

Colin and Michelle, my dearest friends, thank you for being wellsprings of love, support, and faith.

Idil, thank you for your multidimensional perspective, the true laughter we share, the sincere kindness you offer, your thoughtful encouragement, and your honest bravery. And thank you for helping to edit this manuscript from Hvergelmir to Montréal and many, many places in-between!

And, finally, to the lil kings Kamui and Myrlindo, I love you.

About the Author

Danny Sherrard is the founder of Island Verse Literary Collective, a nonprofit organization honoring the voices of the San Juans. He is the youngest person to have won the Individual National Poetry Slam in Austin in 2007 as well as the World Poetry Cup in Paris in 2008. Write Bloody published his first collection of poetry in 2009. Between 2008–2020 Sherrard toured and orchestrated poetry workshops across the United States, Canada, Mexico, and Europe. A Pushcart Prize nominee, his poetry has appeared in numerous publications across the United States and Europe. He is currently putting the finishing touches on his new rendering of the Gilgamesh Epic and is collaborating in many forms of literary magic within the arts community of the San Juan archipelago. islandverse.org

If You Like Danny Sherrard, Danny Likes...

Andrea Gibson

Anis Mojgani

Cristin O'Keefe Aptowicz

Jeffrey McDaniel

Bree Bailey

Write Bloody Publishing publishes and promotes great books of poetry every year.
We believe that poetry can change the world for the better. We are an independent press
dedicated to quality literature and book design, with an office
in Los Angeles, California.

We are grassroots, DIY, bootstrap believers. Pull up a good book and join the family.
Support independent authors, artists, and presses.

Want to know more about Write Bloody books, authors, and events?
Join our mailing list at

www.writebloody.com

WRITE BLOODY BOOKS

After the Witch Hunt — Megan Falley

Aim for the Head: An Anthology of Zombie Poetry — Rob Sturma, Editor

Allow The Light: The Lost Poems of Jack McCarthy — Jessica Lohafer, Editor

Amulet — Jason Bayani

Any Psalm You Want — Khary Jackson

Atrophy — Jackson Burgess

Birthday Girl with Possum — Brendan Constantine

The Bones Below — Sierra DeMulder

Born in the Year of the Butterfly Knife — Derrick C. Brown

Bouquet of Red Flags — Taylor Mali

Bring Down the Chandeliers — Tara Hardy

Ceremony for the Choking Ghost — Karen Finneyfrock

A Constellation of Half-Lives — Seema Reza

Counting Descent — Clint Smith

Courage: Daring Poems for Gutsy Girls — Karen Finneyfrock, Mindy Nettifee, & Rachel McKibbens, Editors

Cut to Bloom — Arhm Choi Wild

Dear Future Boyfriend — Cristin O'Keefe Aptowicz

Do Not Bring Him Water — Caitlin Scarano

Don't Smell the Floss — Matty Byloos

Drive Here and Devastate Me — Megan Falley

Drunks and Other Poems of Recovery — Jack McCarthy

The Elephant Engine High Dive Revival — Derrick C. Brown, Editor

Every Little Vanishing — Sheleen McElhinney

Everyone I Love Is a Stranger to Someone — Annelyse Gelman

Everything Is Everything — Cristin O'Keefe Aptowicz

Favorite Daughter — Nancy Huang

The Feather Room — Anis Mojgani

Floating, Brilliant, Gone — Franny Choi

Glitter in the Blood: A Poet's Manifesto for Better, Braver Writing — Mindy Nettifee

Gold That Frames the Mirror — Brandon Melendez

Open Your Mouth like a Bell — Mindy Nettifee

Ordinary Cruelty — Amber Flame

Our Poison Horse — Derrick C. Brown

Over the Anvil We Stretch — Anis Mojgani

Pansy — Andrea Gibson

Pecking Order — Nicole Homer

The Pocketknife Bible — Anis Mojgani

Pole Dancing to Gospel Hymns — Andrea Gibson

Racing Hummingbirds — Jeanann Verlee

Reasons to Leave the Slaughter — Ben Clark

Redhead and the Slaughter King — Megan Falley

Rise of the Trust Fall — Mindy Nettifee

Said the Manic to the Muse — Jeanann Verlee

Scandalabra — Derrick C. Brown

Slow Dance with Sasquatch — Jeremy Radin

The Smell of Good Mud — Lauren Zuniga

Some of the Children Were Listening — Lauren Sanderson

Songs from Under the River — Anis Mojgani

Strange Light — Derrick C. Brown

The Tigers, They Let Me — Anis Mojgani

Thin Ice Olympics — Jeffery McDaniel

38 Bar Blues — C.R. Avery

This Way to the Sugar — Hieu Minh Nguyen

Time Bomb Snooze Alarm — Bucky Sinister

Uh-Oh — Derrick C. Brown

Uncontrolled Experiments in Freedom — Brian S. Ellis

The Undisputed Greatest Writer of All Time — Beau Sia

The Way We Move Through Water — Lino Anunciacion

We Will Be Shelter — Andrea Gibson, Editor

What Learning Leaves — Taylor Mali

What the Night Demands — Miles Walser

Working Class Represent — Cristin O'Keefe Aptowicz

Workin' Mime to Five — Dick Richards

www.ingramcontent.com/pod-product-compliance
Lightning Source LLC
Chambersburg PA
CBHW031354060726

47590CB00007B/2773